Hey Little Me

Letters to My Inner Child to Heal my Soul

Copyright 2024
Published by Clover Leaf Publications

Contents

Introduction

The lake is so still this morning, like it's waiting for me to speak. I sit on the grass, notebook open in my lap, pen in hand, unsure where to start.

Two years. It's been two years since I lost my husband, and the house is still too quiet. Six months ago, I met someone who made me feel less alone. But when he moved away for work, he didn't ask me to follow. He didn't even hint at it. Another goodbye. Another scar.

My kids are busy with their own lives, far from here, while I'm stuck. Floating.

My therapist says I'm depressed, anxious. She suggested writing to my inner child, connecting with who I was before the heartbreaks, before I became so afraid of love and joy. It sounded silly, but here I am.

"Hey, Little Me…"

The words come slowly. I tell her about the loneliness, the fear, how much I miss feeling carefree. I tell her I'm not sure who I am anymore. When I finish, I tear the page from the notebook, fold it into a paper boat, and place it on the water.

In my mind, I see her—the little girl I used to be—dancing barefoot in the meadow across the lake. She doesn't know loss or fear. She just laughs and spins, her world untouched by scars.

Tears prick my eyes, but I smile for the first time in weeks.

Maybe this isn't so silly after all. Maybe it's a start. As the boat drifts farther away, something inside me loosens. A small knot untangles, leaving behind the faintest flicker of hope.

Maybe this is how I find my way back to her—and to myself.

The First Hello

Hey there, you.

Yeah, you. Sitting over there with your knees pulled up to your chest. I see you peeking out from behind those messy bangs. You don't have to hide, you know. It's just me. Well... it's you too. I'm the older version of you. Kinda weird, huh?

Look, I know we haven't talked much. Okay, we haven't talked at all. I've been... distracted. Grown-up stuff, you know? Paying bills, meeting deadlines, pretending I have it all together. It's exhausting. Honestly, I don't think I've had time to breathe in years.

But today, I sat down and realized something important: I've been missing you. You've been right there, waiting for me to notice, and I didn't. That wasn't fair, was it?

So here I am. Ready to listen.

I want to know everything. Tell me about your favorite game. Is it still pretending to be a pirate sailing across the ocean? Or is it the one where you're the hero saving everyone? Do you still love peanut butter straight from the jar, even when it gets stuck to the roof of your mouth?

I hope you know you're amazing. You've always been. You're brave, curious, and so full of life. Somewhere along the way, I forgot those things about you—about me. But guess what? I'm here now, and I'm ready to remember.

Here's my promise: I'll stop ignoring you. When you feel sad, scared, or even silly, I'll be there. No more leaving you alone to figure things out.

You and me—we're a team now.

So... how about we start with a proper hello?

Hi, little me. I'm so glad I found you.

Love,

Me

Mirror, Mirror

Hey there, little one.

Do you remember that old mirror in Grandma's hallway? The one with the wood frame and the wobbly glass? We used to stare into it, making silly faces and pretending we were famous movie stars. You laughed so much your sides hurt. I loved that sound—your laugh.

But then, something changed.

One day, you looked in the mirror and frowned. Your hair wasn't shiny like the other kids'. Your teeth weren't perfectly straight. You noticed your freckles, and suddenly, they didn't seem so cute anymore. And I? I started to believe all those lies too.

I'm sorry for that.

If I could go back and take your hand, I'd tell you the truth: that mirror was just a piece of glass. It couldn't see your kindness, your bravery, or the way your face lit up when you figured out a hard puzzle. It only showed the outside, and even then, it lied sometimes.

So here's the deal, okay? From now on, we're done with mirrors that make us feel small.

Instead, let's try this: every time we see our reflection, we'll say something nice. "Hey, you look like someone who's about to conquer the world."

Or, "Wow, your eyes are sparkling today!" Let's treat that mirror like a window—a peek into all the magic inside us.

You don't have to believe me yet, but I promise: you are enough. You always have been. Freckles, wobbly teeth, and all.

Next time you see that mirror, blow it a raspberry for me, okay?

Love,

Me

Hopscotch Dreams

Hey there, kiddo.

Remember hopscotch? How you'd draw those squares with chalk, toss a rock, and jump from one to the next, all careful and wobbly on one foot? You used to giggle every time you landed, no matter how shaky the jump.

I've been thinking about that game lately. How simple it was. You never worried about getting it perfect, did you? If you stumbled, you just laughed and tried again.

Somewhere along the way, I forgot how to play like that. These days, every step feels heavy. Every jump feels like it has to land perfectly, or else the whole world will notice.

But maybe we've been looking at things all wrong.

What if life is just one big hopscotch game? Some squares are smooth, others are tricky. Sometimes you'll hit the edge, and yeah, you might even fall. But here's the thing: you don't have to get it perfect. You just have to keep jumping.

Next time I'm scared to take a leap, I'll think of you, skipping along with your wild hair flying everywhere, arms flapping to keep your balance. You didn't care if anyone was watching. You were too busy having fun.

Thanks for showing me how to jump, little me.

Love,

Me

The Puzzle of Us

Hey, little me.

You remember puzzles, don't you? You loved them. You'd sit on the floor for hours, surrounded by all those loose, jumbled pieces. You never seemed to mind the mess. You'd hum a little tune while you searched for the corners, turning each piece over in your tiny hands like it was a treasure.

I've been thinking about those puzzles lately. About how you didn't panic when everything was scattered and incomplete. You knew the picture was in there, even if it didn't look like much at the start. You trusted yourself to put it all back together.

I wish I were more like you.

Now, when life feels like a puzzle, I get overwhelmed. The pieces are everywhere—memories, mistakes, dreams I haven't dared to chase. They're messy and jagged, and some days, it feels like I'll never make sense of them.

But here's what you'd say, isn't it? "Start small. Find the edges. Keep going, even when it's hard."

When you were little, you didn't mind if a piece went missing for a while. You'd keep working until you found it. That patience, that trust—it's something I forgot along the way. I started thinking the puzzle had to be perfect all at once, or it wasn't worth doing at all.

But you remind me that the loose pieces don't mean failure. They're just waiting. They're part of the picture, even when they're not in their place yet.

Thank you for teaching me that. For reminding me that it's okay to take my time. To sit with the mess, to trust that the picture will come together one day.

Let's keep working on this puzzle, piece by piece. We'll find the edges together, okay?

Love,

Me

The Light in the Tunnel

Hey, little me.

Do you remember when we used to hide under the covers with a flashlight? You'd shine it on the pages of your favorite book, the beam lighting up the words like they were magic. I used to think you weren't afraid of anything. Even when the room was dark, you'd create your own little world of light.

But I know now that wasn't true. You were scared sometimes—of the dark, of being alone, of things not turning out the way you hoped. You just didn't let it stop you. You always looked for the light, even when it was hard to find.

I need to tell you something: I forget that now. When things feel dark, I lose the flashlight. I sit in the shadows, waiting for the light to find me. But you—oh, you—taught me that the light doesn't come on its own. You have to look for it, make it, shine it yourself if you have to.

So that's what I'm going to do. I'll remember what it felt like to crawl into a blanket fort, click on that flashlight, and make the whole world glow again. I'll remind myself that even the tiniest beam can cut through the darkest night.

Thank you for teaching me how to find the light, even when it feels like there's none to be found.

Let's hold the flashlight together this time, okay?

Love,

Me

Threads of Love

Hey there, little one.

Do you remember those summer afternoons in the backyard? You'd find bits of string, ribbons, or whatever you could, and you'd weave them between the branches of trees. You'd call it your "love web," remember? You said it connected everything so the trees wouldn't feel lonely, so they'd know they belonged to each other.

I didn't understand it then. I thought it was just another one of your silly games. But now, I see how wise you were.

You knew what love really meant. It wasn't loud or flashy. It was quiet, steady—like those threads you strung up. It was about connection. About making sure no one felt alone.

Somewhere along the way, I got caught up in thinking love was supposed to be big, dramatic, perfect. I forgot about the simple beauty of it. The kind you knew, the kind that just... is.

I want to weave threads like you did. Not just for trees, but for the people in my life. To let them know they're not alone, that they belong, that someone cares.

Thank you for teaching me that love isn't something you wait for. It's something you create, one little thread at a time.

I'll start weaving again, just like you.

Love,

Me

The Tightest Hugs

"Hey, little me.

Do you remember how you used to hug? You'd throw your whole self into it, arms stretched wide, running full speed toward your friends. You hugged like you were afraid they might slip away if you didn't hold on tight enough. And they'd laugh, sometimes squeal, but they'd hug you back just as fiercely.

Love was simple back then. Pure. Honest. It didn't ask for anything in return, and it didn't hide. You just loved, completely.

I don't love like that anymore.

Because somewhere along the way, love started to hurt. The disappointments came first—small cracks that made me hesitate. Then there were betrayals and lies, sharp enough to cut deep. And every time, I'd patch the hurt with a band aid.

 I told myself, "Don't let it show. You'll be fine."

But band aids don't make things disappear, do they? They just cover up the wounds long enough for them to scar.

And scars—scars are tough. They're a reminder of what hurt, of what healed, but they're never soft again. They can't bend the way unbroken skin does. They stay.

I wish I could hug the way you did. With open arms and no fear of breaking. But now, every hug feels cautious, careful, afraid of what might go wrong. Scars make you wary, don't they? They whisper, "Be careful—this might hurt again.

"I want to remember your way of loving. Of trusting. Of throwing your arms wide and letting the world in, scars and all. I don't know if I can ever be as fearless as you, but maybe I can try.

Even if the scars stay, maybe love can still stretch around them.

Love,

Me

Seeds of Hope

Hey, little me.

Do you remember planting seeds in the garden? You'd poke your tiny finger into the dirt, drop in a seed, and cover it up like you were tucking it into bed. Then you'd water it—too much, most of the time—and check on it every day, waiting for the first little sprout to peek through.

You never doubted it would grow. Even when the days stretched on with no sign of life, you still believed. You'd say, "It just needs more time," like you understood something I've forgotten.

I think about those seeds now, how small they were. How easily they could've been stepped on or forgotten. But you never stopped caring for them. You believed in what they could become.

I wish I could be like that again. These days, it feels like hope is hard to plant. The world feels big and heavy, and it's hard to believe that something so small could make a difference. I get impatient, doubting whether anything will ever grow.

But you remind me that it's not about seeing results right away. It's about having the courage to plant the seed in the first place. It's about trusting that, even if you don't see it yet, something is happening beneath the surface.

So I'm going to start planting again. Little seeds of hope, one at a time. Maybe it'll take a while to see them grow. Maybe I'll need to be patient. But I'll trust the way you did.

Love,

Me

The Day the World Stopped

Hey, Little Me,

 I want to tell you about the day my world stopped. It was a Tuesday. The sun was shining like it always did, like it didn't know. How could it know? Everything looked the same, but everything was different.

He was gone. The man who made me laugh until my stomach hurt. The one who knew what I needed without me saying a word. The one who held my hand in the dark, the one I thought I'd have forever with—just... gone.

 I remember the way the nurse looked at me. Her words were soft, careful, but they still broke me. I remember collapsing on the hospital floor, gasping for air. I remember screaming in my head, begging for it not to be true. But it was. It was true.

I wish you could have been there, Little Me. Not because I'd ever want you to feel that kind of pain—I wouldn't. But because I needed someone. I needed you.

I've been carrying that day ever since. The weight of it. The sharp edges of it. I tried to bury it, to move forward, to forget how it felt. But it doesn't go away, does it? It just lingers.

You're crying now. I see your little face, the tears streaming down your cheeks. I didn't want to make you sad, but I had to tell you. I had to let you see the part of me I've been hiding.

And now you're hugging me, wrapping your little arms around me so tight I can barely breathe. I didn't know I needed that. But I do.

Thank you, Little Me. For being here. For holding me. For reminding me it's okay to cry.

Maybe now, I can finally let this part of me heal.

Love,

Me

The Gift of Freedom

Hey, Little Me,

Thank you. I don't even know where to start, except to say that. Thank you for being here. For holding me, for letting me cry. I've been holding onto that day for so long, the day I lost him. I've carried it like a weight I thought I'd never set down. But when you hugged me, it was like some of that heaviness slipped away.

You didn't say anything, but you didn't have to. You reminded me that it's okay to feel, to let the sadness come and go. You reminded me that I'm not alone, even when it feels like I am.

And now, sitting here by the lake, I feel something I haven't felt in a long time. It's small, like a tiny crack of sunlight breaking through the clouds, but it's there: relief.

Do you remember how you used to run through the field, arms stretched out like you were flying? You'd laugh so hard you'd trip over your own feet, but you'd get right back up and keep going. You weren't scared of falling. You didn't think about who was watching or if you looked silly. You just ran.

I miss that. I miss you.

So, maybe it's time. Time to let go of some of the things I've been carrying. Time to stretch my arms wide, feel the wind on my face, and remember what it feels like to be free.

I'm not there yet, but I'll get there. And when I do, I'll run like you did. Thank you, Little Me, for showing me how to take that first step.

Love,

Me

A New Chapter Begins

Evening Diary Entry

Hey, Little Me,

It's funny—I used to think the hardest part of this would be starting. But here I am, sitting in bed with my new diary, and I'm realizing the hardest part is admitting I need to change.

When I wrote to you earlier by the lake, something shifted. It wasn't dramatic—there wasn't some magical lightning bolt of clarity—but for the first time in ages, I felt... lighter. It's like you hugged the part of me that's been hurting for so long and whispered, It's okay. Let go.

So, I've decided: no more hiding. No more letting grief wrap around me like a blanket I can't escape. I'm done being afraid to live, afraid to feel.

Today, I looked in the mirror, really looked, and saw a woman I barely recognized. She's tired, yes, but she's still here. I'm still here. And that has to mean something, doesn't it?

I'm going to make a change, Little Me. Not tomorrow. Not next week. Right now.

First, I'm going to stop letting this grief control me. I've been trapped in it for too long, and I'm tired of feeling stuck. Tomorrow, I'm going to do something just for me. I'll call that old salon downtown and get my hair done. And then, I'll call Denise—you remember her, don't you? She always had that big laugh, the one that made everyone feel warm inside. I'm going to ask her to go out with me.

It doesn't have to be big. Maybe a coffee. Maybe a play. It doesn't matter. What matters is I'm moving forward.

And you know what? I realized something today. I don't need to find love. I don't need someone to save me. Maybe—just maybe—I need to give love instead.

I think I know what I need to do. But for now, one step at a time.

Goodnight, Little Me. Thank you for helping me see it's not too late. I'm not too old. I'm only 67, after all. And I still have so much life left to live.

Love, me, Gloria

The Mirror Smiles Back

Evening Journal Entry

Hey, Little Me,

Today, I walked into that salon with my heart pounding. I almost didn't go in. For years, I've avoided mirrors, avoided myself. What if I didn't like what I saw? But then I thought of you, and I knew I had to try.

Lydia, the stylist, greeted me with a big smile and didn't ask any questions. She just sat me down, wrapped me in that cape, and started snipping. At first, I couldn't bring myself to look in the mirror. My reflection felt like a stranger, someone I wasn't ready to face.

But as she worked, something shifted. Strands of hair fell to the floor, taking years of neglect with them. My reflection changed, bit by bit, and I couldn't help but steal glances. That tired, invisible woman I'd been avoiding started to fade, and someone else began to emerge—someone I hadn't seen in a long time.

When Lydia finished, she turned me to the mirror. And there I was.

My hair was soft, framing my face like sunlight through a window. My eyes looked brighter, my cheeks fuller. I smiled—not out of politeness, but because I wanted to. And in that smile, I saw you, Little Me. The girl who ran barefoot in the fields, laughed freely, and wasn't afraid to take up space.

I walked out of that salon feeling alive. I called Denise, and tonight we went to see a play. I laughed so hard I cried—happy tears this time.

Thank you, Little Me, for reminding me that I'm still here. I see you. I see us.

Love,

Gloria

Back to the Classroom

Evening Journal Entry

Hey, Little Me,

Today, I walked into a place I thought I'd never return to: the school where I used to teach.

The smell of crayons and chalk dust hit me the moment I walked in, and it was like stepping back into another life. I felt my heart pound as I approached the office, my palms sweaty, my mind racing with questions. Would they even want me back? Did I still have what it takes?

But then I thought of you. I thought of your curious little face, the way you used to light up when you learned something new, and it gave me the courage to step inside.

Mrs. Bradley, the principal, looked surprised to see me, but her face softened as I explained why I was there. I told her I wanted to come back, even if just part-time. I admitted how much I missed the children, the energy of the classroom, and the way teaching made me feel alive.

She smiled—really smiled—and said, "Gloria, we'd love to have you back."

I felt tears sting my eyes, but this time, they weren't from sadness. As she showed me around the school, I saw children running down the hallways, their laughter echoing everywhere. I peeked into a classroom and saw their little faces, so full of wonder. And in that moment, I knew: this was where I was meant to be.

Thank you, Little Me, for pushing me to find my courage. I feel like I've taken another step closer to you—and to myself.

Love,

Gloria

A Hopscotch Heart

Evening Journal Entry

Hey, Little Me,

I played hopscotch today.

I didn't plan to—it just sort of happened. Recess was buzzing, the kids were running around, and I stood there watching, soaking it all in. Then one of them ran up to me, this sweet little girl with pigtails and a mischievous grin, and said, "Miss Gloria, come play!"

I almost said no. I almost told her that teachers don't play hopscotch, that I'd embarrass myself, that I was too old. But then I heard your voice. You whispered, "Why not?"

So, I kicked off my shoes and jumped into the first square. The kids cheered, and I laughed—really laughed—as I hopped, stumbled, and almost fell over. They giggled and clapped, and for a moment, I felt like one of them.

The sun was shining, my cheeks were flushed, and for the first time in years, I felt light. Free.

It wasn't just a game, Little Me. It was a reminder. A reminder that joy doesn't have to be big or complicated. It can be as simple as jumping on chalk-drawn squares with kids who see the world as you used to: a place full of possibilities.

And you know what? It didn't matter that my legs wobbled or that my jumps weren't perfect. What mattered was that I tried. What mattered was that I felt alive.

Thank you, Little Me, for giving me back this piece of myself.

Love,

Gloria

The Art of Joy

Evening Journal Entry

Hey, Little Me,

Today was one of those days that fills your heart without warning.

The kids were restless after lunch, their energy bubbling over like a shaken soda can. Instead of trying to rein them in, I decided to let them loose in the best way I could think of: art.

I pulled out every scrap of paper, every marker, crayon, and paintbrush I could find. "Let's make something beautiful," I said. They stared at me for a moment, then dove in, their little hands reaching for supplies.

And oh, Little Me, you would have loved it. The room turned into a swirl of colors and laughter. One boy painted a dragon breathing rainbow fire. A girl made a flower bigger than her whole sheet of paper. They asked me to join in, and for the first time in years, I picked up a paintbrush.

I painted you. Not perfectly, of course, but I painted the little girl who ran barefoot in the fields, the girl who laughed without fear, the girl who reminded me to live again.

When the bell rang, the kids didn't want to leave. They stood proudly by their creations, chattering about their ideas and what they'd do next time. As I cleaned up, I looked at the colorful chaos around me—the smudges of paint, the paper scraps—and I felt... alive.

Joy doesn't have to be loud or perfect, does it? Sometimes, it's in the messy moments, the ones filled with color and life.

Thank you, Little Me, for showing me that again.

Love, Gloria

GLORIA

The Christmas Play

Evening Journal Entry

Hey, Little Me,

It's funny how life can surprise you, isn't it?

You know I've been working part-time at the school, which has been wonderful. But lately, I've found myself spending more and more time at the church. I started going just to sit in the back, to feel something bigger than myself. Then one day, I overheard the pastor talking about how they needed someone to help with the children's Christmas play. Before I even realized what I was doing, I volunteered.

Little Me, you would've loved it. The church hall has been alive with laughter and energy these past weeks. I've been sewing angel costumes, wrangling wiggly shepherds, and teaching carols to a choir of giggling little ones. It's messy and chaotic, but it feels like home.

Tonight was the big night—the play we've been working so hard on. The children stepped onto the little stage in the church hall, their faces glowing under the warm lights. The nativity scene unfolded with all the sweetness and silliness you'd expect—an angel tripping on her robe, a wise man dropping his gift—but none of it mattered.

The church was packed with families, the tree twinkled with lights, and for the first time in years, I felt... complete. I didn't realize how much I missed being part of something bigger than myself, how much I needed this sense of community.

Thank you, Little Me, for reminding me how good it feels to give, to be part of something joyful.

Merry Christmas, Little Me.

Love,

Gloria

A Christmas to Remember

Evening Journal Entry

Hey, Little Me,

I don't even know where to begin. Tonight feels like a dream, one of those magical, impossible things you see in movies and never think will happen to you. But it did. It really did.

The Christmas play was beautiful. The children were absolutely perfect in their wonderfully imperfect way. Angels with tilted halos, shepherds trying not to giggle, and that sweet little wise man carrying his gift upside down the entire time—it was all so charming. The parents clapped, the tree sparkled, and for a moment, I just sat there and soaked it all in.

It felt like everything had come full circle. The laughter, the joy, the sense of belonging—I'd almost forgotten how much I needed it. For the first time in years, I felt complete.

And then my phone buzzed.

I nearly ignored it, but something told me to answer. "Hello?" I whispered, trying not to disrupt the hum of chatter around me.

"Gloria, it's me. Bob."

I froze. His voice. After all these months, there it was, warm and familiar, like a song I hadn't heard in forever but still knew by heart.

"Bob?" I barely managed to get the word out.

"I'm home," he said softly. "I've missed you so much.

"I couldn't speak. My heart was pounding, my mind racing. And then I looked up, and there he was. Standing in the aisle of the church, holding a bouquet of red Christmas flowers, smiling at me like I was the only person in the world.

I stood, my hands trembling as he walked toward me. The chatter around us quieted, and suddenly it felt like we were the only two people in the room.

A Christmas to Remember (continued)

"Gloria," he began, his voice steady but full of emotion. "I'm sorry. I shouldn't have left without asking you. I thought Alaska would be too hard for you, with your arthritis, and I didn't want to burden you. But the truth is, being away from you was harder than anything else."

Tears stung my eyes. I couldn't believe what I was hearing.

"I quit," he continued. "I came back because I realized something. I don't care where I work or what I do—I just want to be near you. You look so radiant, so happy, and I want to be part of this life you've built."

Before I could even process his words, he got down on one knee.

Little Me, my heart nearly stopped.

The room gasped, and then one of the children, sweet and innocent, shouted, "Say yes! Say yes!" The parents joined in, clapping and chanting, "Say yes!"

I felt my cheeks burn with embarrassment, but I couldn't stop smiling. Bob held out a ring, his eyes shining with love. "Gloria," he said, "will you marry me?"

I laughed through my tears, covering my mouth with one hand while the other reached for his. "Yes,"

I whispered, and then louder, so everyone could hear. "Yes!"

The room erupted into cheers. Bob stood, pulling me into his arms, and before I knew it, we were kissing, surrounded by applause and laughter. The children danced, the parents smiled, and the Christmas tree seemed to twinkle a little brighter.

I can't believe it, Little Me. For so long, I thought love was something I didn't deserve anymore. But tonight, I realized something. Love doesn't have an expiration date. It grows, it changes, and sometimes, it finds you when you least expect it.

Thank you, Little Me, for helping me find my joy again.

Merry Christmas,

Gloria

Our Publications

Visit our website at:

https/cloverleaf.pub for our entire
catalog of publications.
We add new publications regularly.